DUAL MOMENTUM TREND TRADING

Also by Lee Tang

Dual Momentum Trend Trading
Canada's Public Pension System Made Simple
Summary & Study Guide Series:

Brain Maker
The Gene
The Emperor of All Maladies
NeuroTribes
Brain Storms
The End of Diabetes
The End of Heart Disease
ADHD Nation
The Obesity Code
How Not to Die
Mind over Meds
A Crack in Creation
The Gene Machine
The Body Builders
Into the Gary Zone
Fat for Fuel
The Alzheimer's Solution
Healing Arthritis
Rise of the Necrofauna
We Are Our Brains
The Teenage Brain
The Better Brain Solution
The Plant Paradox
The Fountain
Resurrection Science
Sapiens
Homo Deus

The Beautiful Cure
The Diabetes Code
Brain Food
Anticancer Living
The End of Epidemics
The Rise and Fall of the Dinosaurs
10% Human
The Mind-Gut Connection
Civilization Microbia
An Elegant Defense
Cancerland
Empty Planet
The Longevity Paradox
Eat to Beat Disease
The Tangled Tree
The Body
The Spectrum of Hope
Memory Rescue
The Longevity Code
Healing Anxiety and Depression
Healing ADD/ADHD
The Telomere Miracle
The Finance Curse

For a complete list of books by Lee Tang and information about the author, visit LMTPRESS.WORDPRESS.COM.

Get Access to the Best Trading Strategy Available today!

Here is a simple and reliable method to make money in stock, ETF, futures, and forex markets without quitting your day job.

This book offers you a simple and reliable trading system that you can use right away with no guessing or tweaking required. It comes with a trend filter that helps you to understand the strength of the existing trend, and a momentum filter that you can tweak to fit your own trading style and to increase its robustness.

The mechanics of this system were first unveiled in a public forum several years ago. The author takes it to the next level by using daily charts as the primary trading time frame and adding a trend and momentum filter. If you follow this system correctly, you will be taking only high probability trades. The system will keep you in the trade for as long as the trend is running strong so that you will not be leaving money on the table by exiting too soon. With this system in your trading arsenal, you will not be making the mistakes most traders make, especially over-trading and over-analyzing, the main reasons why most traders are not profitable.

This book is a must-read for anyone starting their journey into trading, or even experienced traders who are not getting the results they want from trading. It is ideal for people who work full time or those with busy schedules. You'll learn how successful traders make money by consistently trading trends—and how you can copy that success.

This book is short and can be easily finished within a couple of hours. It provides simple and easy to follow trading rules, and can dramatically change your financial prospects! For less than what you would pay in commission on one trade, this book would be the best investment (of money and time) you have ever made.

If you want to fast-forward your learning curve and learn to trade effectively as quickly as possible, read this book and give yourself a head start against the 90% of traders who consistently lose.

DUAL MOMENTUM TREND TRADING

How to Avoid Costly Trading Mistakes and Make More Money in the Stock, ETF, Futures, and Forex Markets with This Simple and Reliable Swing Trading Strategy

Lee Tang

Title: Dual Momentum Trend Trading
Subtitle: How to Avoid Costly Trading Mistakes and Make More Money in the Stock, ETF, Futures and Forex Markets with This Simple and Reliable Swing Trading Strategy
Author: Lee Tang
Publisher: LMT Press (lmtpress.wordpress.com)

Copyright © 2015 by Lee Tang

All rights reserved. Aside from brief quotations for media coverage and reviews, no part of this book may be reproduced or distributed in any form without the author's permission. Thank you for supporting authors and a diverse, creative culture by purchasing this book and complying with copyright laws.

First Edition: March 2015
Issued in print and electronic formats.
ISBN 9780995943148 (ebook)
ISBN 9781548201012 (paperback)

Limit of Liability/Disclaimer of Warranty: The publisher and author make no representations or warranties regarding the accuracy or completeness of these contents and disclaim all warranties such as warranties of fitness for a particular purpose. The website addresses in the book were correct at the time going to print. However, the publisher and author are not responsible for the content of third-party websites, which are subject to change.

To my wife, Lillian, who is the source of energy and love for everything I do, and to Andrew and Amanda: watching you grow up has been a privilege.

Disclaimer

By reading this book, you acknowledge that trading is risky and you could have substantial losses that exceed your capital investment. Trading financial instruments profitably is very difficult and is not for everyone.

This is an informational book and nothing associated with it should be construed as specific advice to buy or sell (or not buy or sell) any financial instruments, or be implied to guarantee profitable trading. No one associated with it accepts any liability for any losses or damages relating to any content here. Any mention of trades in financial instruments should be assumed to be hypothetical.

We recommend that you consult with a licensed, qualified professional before making any investment decisions. It is your responsibility to perform due diligence regarding all trades and entities with which you do business.

Contents

Preface: Why I Wrote This Book..xi

Introduction: Why You Should Read This Book....................1

    1. Market Structure 101...3

    2. Choosing the Proper Trading Time Frame..................9

    3. Setting Up Your Charts...11

    4. How I Use the Indicators...15

    5. The Strategy – Methodology......................................25

    6. The Strategy - Trading Rules......................................27

    7. Diversification and Position Sizing............................33

    8. Finding the Best Market to Trade..............................35

    9. Putting It All Together..39

What Next?..41

About the Author...43

Preface
Why I Wrote This Book

TREND TRADING IS a popular strategy used by many new and experienced traders because of its simplicity. In a nutshell, the strategy requires you to look at the charts and recognize trends. Once you've established that there is a trend, you buy dips on an uptrend and sell rallies on a downtrend. Statistically speaking, the trend will continue and you will make a profit.

If trading is that simple, how come over 90 percent of traders are not successful? Here are the main reasons: how come over 90 percent of traders are not successful? Here are the main reasons:

- *Trading without a plan.*
- *Buying dips* (or selling rallies) blindly—not realizing the trend is ending.
- *Taking profits too soon*—leaving too much money on the table.
- *Exiting too late*—slow to exit when the trend reverses.
- *Trading against the dominant trend.*
- *Trading on small time frames*—small time frame traders tend to over-trade and over-analyze and are more exposed to whipsaws and shakeouts from intraday market noise that is almost impossible to predict.

I have made all these mistakes in the past and want no other aspiring traders to go through the struggles I went through! I wrote this book for traders like you who want to learn how to trade using a profitable trading strategy that is robust enough to prevent the trader from making these costly mistakes. I have written this book because I wish I had something like this years ago when I started trading.

Introduction
Why You Should Read This Book

This book gives you a simple and reliable trading system you can use right away with no guessing or tweaking required. The basic system was first unveiled on a public forum several years ago and this book takes it to the next level by using daily charts as the primary trading time frame and adding a trend and momentum filter. If you follow this system correctly, you will be taking high probability trades only. The system will keep you in the trade for as long as the trend is intact, so you will not be leaving money on the table by exiting too soon. With this system in your trading arsenal, you will not be making the mistakes most traders make, i.e., over-trading and over-analyzing, which are the main reasons most traders are not profitable.

This book is a must-read for anyone starting their journey into trading or even experienced traders not getting the results they want from trading. It is ideal for people working full time or those with a busy schedule.

In this book, you will learn how a successful trader makes money consistently trading trends and how you can copy that success. Specifically, you will learn:

❏ How to choose the right time frame to trade.

- ❑ How to tell whether the market is trending and whether the existing trend is (a) stable and strong or (b) about to end.
- ❑ How to enter a trade only when the trend is strong and exit a trade only when the trend is about to end.
- ❑ How to maximize your profit by aligning market cycles, momentum, and trends across multiple time frames.
- ❑ How to pick a direction to trade so you won't be trading against the dominant trend.
- ❑ How to manage risks by diversifying and position sizing your trading portfolio.
- ❑ How to scan the market to find the best securities to trade.

The trading rules are simple and easy to follow. The book is short and can be easily finished within two hours. For a cost less than the commission on one trade, you will find this book the best investment (of money and time) you have ever made. If you want to fast-forward your learning curve and learn to trade effectively quickly, read this book and give yourself a head start against the 90 percent of traders who consistently lose.

Chapter 1
Market Structure 101

This chapter introduces basic concepts for beginning traders. Experienced traders are welcome to skip to the next chapter.

Market Trends

A trend is a general direction in which a security or market is headed. A market can trend in one of three directions—up, down, or sideways. An uptrend is defined by a series of higher highs and higher lows, while a downtrend is defined by a series of lower highs and lower lows. A sideways trend occurs when a market trades in a fixed range and makes little progress up or down.

Figure 1: Types of Trend

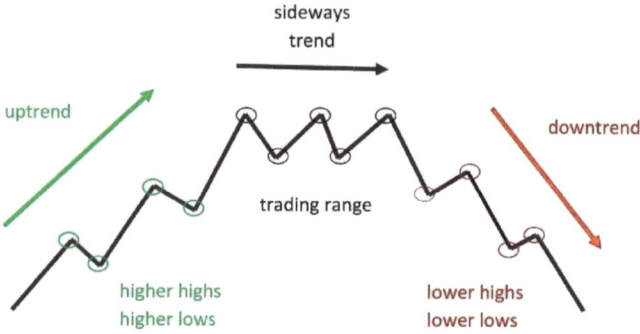

Trends occur when the market is absorbing new information and the market participants are re-pricing the asset. However, not all market participants are the same. They all react differently to the new information and make trading decisions based on different time horizons. The time horizon for a short-term trader is entirely different from that of an institutional investor. For a short-term trader, the time horizon can be from several minutes up to several days while, for the investor, it's 12 to 18 months. Asset prices reflect a combination of short-term technical trading and long-term fundamental valuations. Short-term price changes are likely to be more volatile than longer-term trends. The underlying trend in the market reflects the changes in expected earnings, based on the changing economic environment. Short-term trends are more likely the result of crowd behavior.

The Fractal Nature of Trends

- Trends occur in all time frames.
- Every time frame has its own structure.
- The higher time frames overrule the lower time frames.
- A trend in motion is more likely to continue than to reverse.
- Trend reversal comes from the inside out—trend reversal starts from lower time frames and propagates to higher time frames.

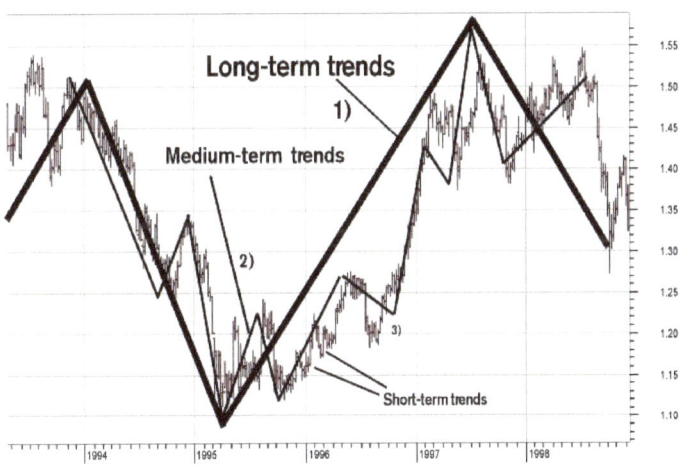

Figure 2: Fractal Nature of Trends

In Chapter 4, I will describe how to use a simple indicator to recognize trends and determine if the existing trend is (a) stable and strong, or (b) about to end.

Market Cycles

All markets are cyclical. They go up, peak, then bottom. When one cycle is finished, the next begins. The chart represents a cycle in a sine wave. It also shows the different stages of market activity in one market cycle. During the trough, stocks are accumulated and will be marked-up on the way up. At the peak, stocks will be distributed, and when done it's time to markdown their prices and the cycle will begin anew again.

Figure 3: Market Cycle

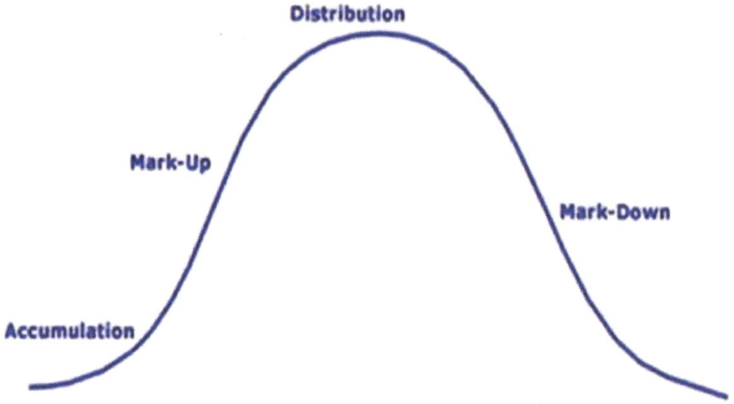

Market cycles are also fractal. Within each cycle, you will find smaller sub-cycles. A cycle can last anywhere from a few weeks to several years, depending on the nature of the market and the time horizon at which you are looking. A day trader using five-minute bars may see four complete cycles per day while, for a long-term investor, a cycle may last for months or years. An understanding of cycles is essential if you want to maximize investment or trading returns.

The Fractal Nature of Trends

- Trends occur in all time frames.
- Every time frame has its own structure.
- The higher time frames overrule the lower time frames.
- A trend in motion is more likely to continue than to reverse.
- Trend reversal comes from the inside out—trend reversal starts from lower time frames and propagates to higher time frames.

Figure 2: Fractal Nature of Trends

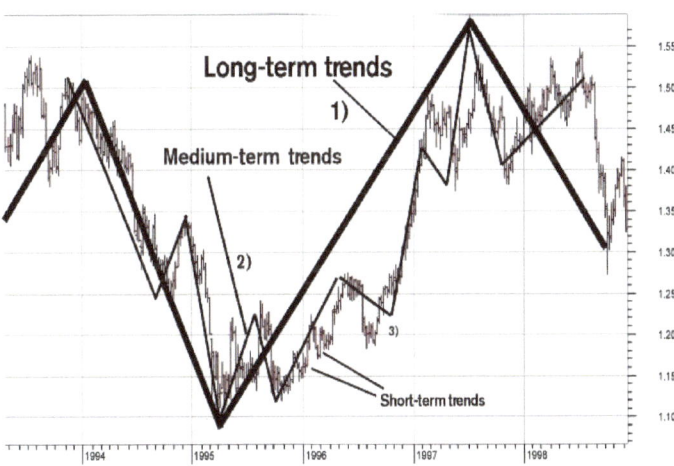

In Chapter 4, I will describe how to use a simple indicator to recognize trends and determine if the existing trend is (a) stable and strong, or (b) about to end.

Market Cycles

All markets are cyclical. They go up, peak, then bottom. When one cycle is finished, the next begins. The chart represents a cycle in a sine wave. It also shows the different stages of market activity in one market cycle. During the trough, stocks are accumulated and will be marked-up on the way up. At the peak, stocks will be distributed, and when done it's time to markdown their prices and the cycle will begin anew again.

Figure 3: Market Cycle

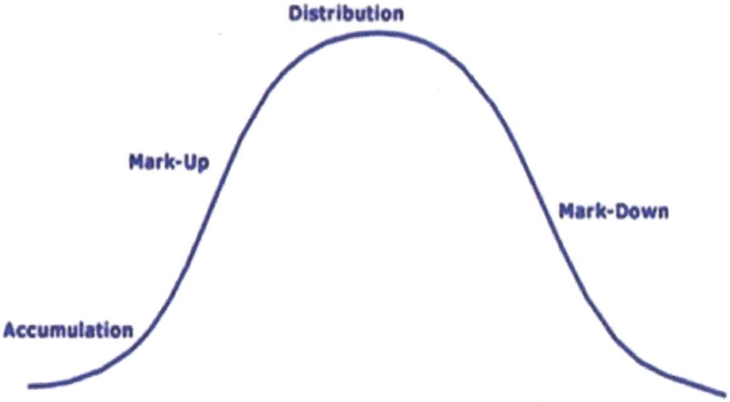

Market cycles are also fractal. Within each cycle, you will find smaller sub-cycles. A cycle can last anywhere from a few weeks to several years, depending on the nature of the market and the time horizon at which you are looking. A day trader using five-minute bars may see four complete cycles per day while, for a long-term investor, a cycle may last for months or years. An understanding of cycles is essential if you want to maximize investment or trading returns.

Figure 4: Market Cycle Model

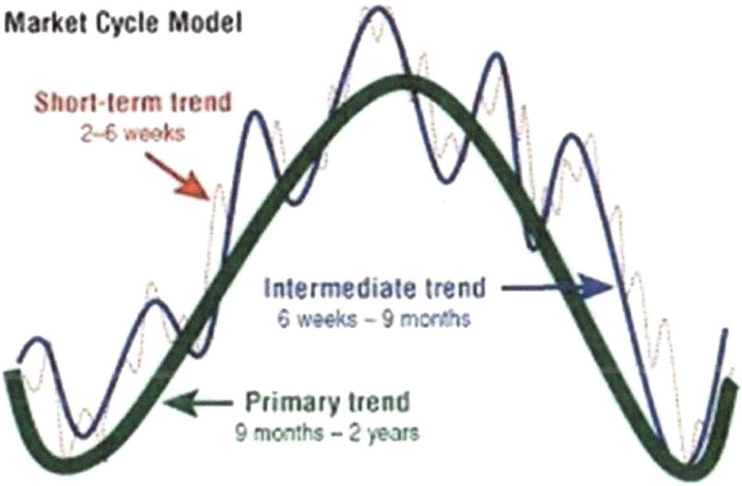

Market Cycle Model

Short-term trend
2–6 weeks

Intermediate trend
6 weeks – 9 months

Primary trend
9 months – 2 years

Chapter 2
Choosing the Proper Trading Time Frame

If you are trading using a time frame lower than the daily time frame, you will be exposed to these trading problems:

- **Over-trading**—Most traders over-trade from focusing on lower time frames. Daily charts help inhibit over-trading because you get fewer signals, but they are more accurate.
- **Fear of placing trades**—Not focusing on the daily charts as your primary technical analysis time frame usually leads to confusion, indecision, and ultimately fear. You will feel unconfident about which trades to take and which to pass on, like a deer caught in the headlights.
- **Over-analyzing**—The daily chart gives us the most pertinent view of the market. So, if you are not focused on the daily chart, you are probably spending too much time on other less-pertinent market variables. This will confuse you and cause you to enter trades based more on "guessing" than anything else.
- **Addiction to trading**—Many traders often forget higher time frames are more accurate. They spend countless hours analyzing their trades, checking intraday charts at work, and constantly thinking about the markets.

- **Trading inconsistently**—Trading signals are stronger and clearer on daily charts than on intraday charts. Your trading will be more profitable and consistent due to the increased reliability of the signals. Trading with signals from intraday charts can make your trading inconsistent due to intraday market noise.

We will be using daily charts as the primary trading time frame in this book.

Chapter 3
Setting Up Your Charts

Guppy Multiple Moving Averages (GMMA)

THIS INDICATOR WAS invented by Daryl Guppy. Your charting platform might have this indicator in their indicator library. Few do. Fortunately, you can add it to your charts easily because it is just a collection of 12 *exponential moving averages* of various lengths. Exponential moving average (*EMA*) is a type of moving average like a simple moving average, except that more weight is given to the latest data. This moving average reacts faster to recent price changes than a simple moving average and is a common indicator available in all charting platform.

The *GMMA* indicator is constructed from two groups of moving averages:

- The *short-term GMMA* consists of the 3, 5, 8, 10, 12 and 15 day EMA. We will color them blue.
- The *Long-term GMMA* consists of the 30, 35, 40, 45, 50 and 60 day EMA. We will color them red.

The Full Stochastic Oscillator

The *Full Stochastic Oscillator* was developed by George Lane in the 1950's. It is a momentum indicator designed to show the relation of the close price relative to the high/low range over several prior periods using a scale of 0-100. In this trading strategy, we will be using two stochastic oscillators, one long-term and one short-term.

Settings for long-term STO
- Overbought =80
- Oversold = 20
- K-period=20
- d-period=3
- slowing period=8;
- average type =SMA

Settings for short-term STO
- Overbought =80
- Oversold = 20
- K-period=5
- d-period=3
- slowing period=2;
- average type =SMA

The Relative Strength Index (RSI)

The relative strength index was developed by J. Welles Wilder and published in a 1978 book, *New Concepts in Technical Trading Systems*. The RSI is a momentum oscillator which computes momentum as the ratio of higher closes to lower closes. We use the following setting for the indicator:

Settings for RSI
- length=7
- overbought=50
- oversold=50

200 Exponential Moving Average (200 EMA)

This is the 200-day exponential moving average.

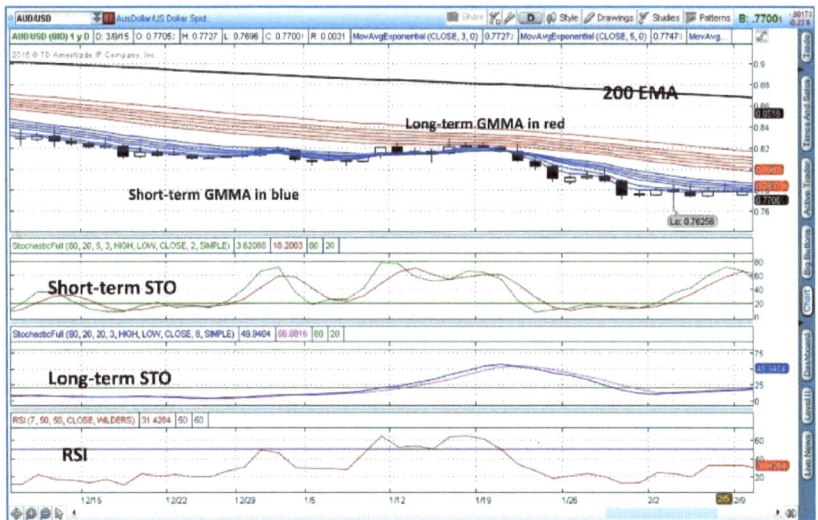

Figure 5: Required Indicators

Table 1: Summary of Indicator Settings		
Indicator	Settings	Remarks
Short-term GMMA	3, 5, 8, 10, 12, and 15 day EMA	Blue
Long-term GMMA	30, 35, 40, 45, 50, and 60 day EMA	Red
Short-term STO	OB=80; OS=20; K-period=5; d-period=3; slowing period=2; average type=SMA	OB= overbought OS = oversold
Long-term STO	OB=80; OS=20; K-period=20; d-period=3; slowing period=8; average type=SMA	Green if >=50 Red if <50
RSI	Length=7; OB=50; OS=50	Major S/R
200 EMA	200-day exponential moving average	

Chapter 4
How I Use the Indicators

WE USE THE Guppy Multiple Moving Average (GMMA) indicators as a trend filter for the strategy:

- The short-term GMMA is used to analyze the secondary trend.
- The long-term GMMA is used to analyze the primary trend.

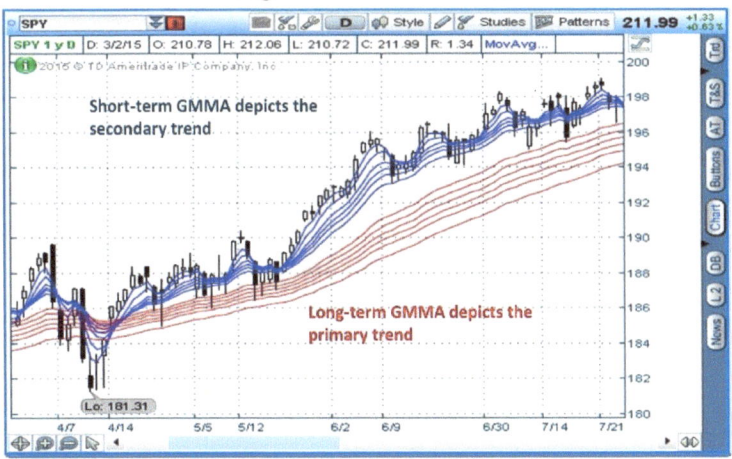

Figure 6: Guppy Multiple Moving Average Indicator
Short-term GMMAs in blue
Long-term GMMAs in red

We look for patterns on this indicator to find clues as to (1) whether the market is trending, and (2) whether the existing trend is strong or weak.

Angle and Separation

- The angles (slopes) and separation of the moving averages within the short-term GMMAs depict the direction of the secondary trend. If the angle is pointing up and the moving averages are separated from each other, then the secondary trend is up. If it's pointing down and the moving averages are separated from each other, then the secondary trend is down. Otherwise, it is mixed.
- The angles (slopes) and separation of the moving averages within the long-term GMMAs depict the direction of the primary trend. If the angle is pointing up and the moving averages are separated from each other, then the primary trend is up. If it's pointing down and the moving averages are separated from each other, then the primary trend is down. Otherwise, it is mixed.
- The market is in an uptrend if the long-term GMMAs all have good upward angles and are separated, and the short-term GMMAs are all lying above the long-term GMMAs with good separation between the two groups.
- The market is in a downtrend if the long-term GMMAs all have good downward angles and are separated, and the short-term GMMAs are all lying below the long-term GMMAs with good separation between the two groups.
- In Figure 7, the long-term GMMAs are all angling up and separated. The short-term GMMAs are all above the long-term GMMAs with good separation between the two groups. This confirms an uptrend.
- The trend for the market is mixed if there is no separation between the two groups of GMMAs, i.e. if the blue moving averages cut into the red moving averages. See the circled part on the lower left corner of Figure 7.

How I Use the Indicators | 17

Figure 7: Angle and Separation Confirms a Trend

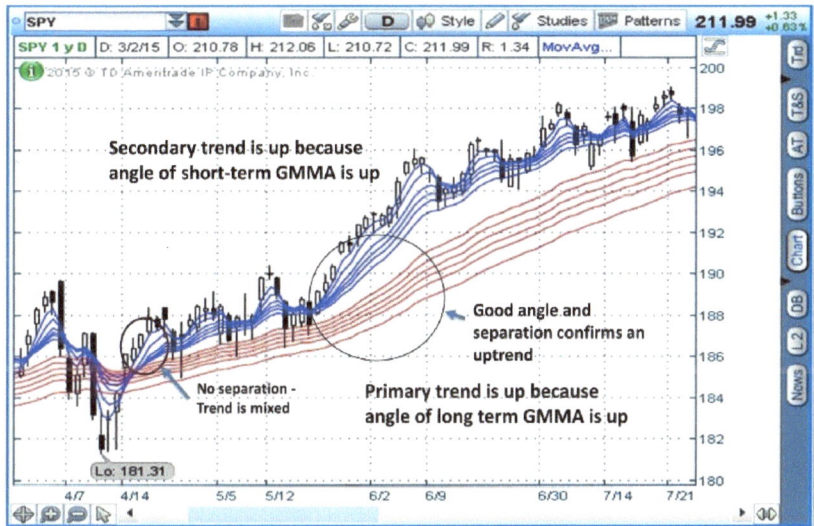

Compressions and Expansions

- ❏ Periods of compression of the short-term GMMAs (when the GMMAs narrow down) suggest that the secondary trend momentum is fading. This happens when price is undergoing short-term "correction."
- ❏ Periods of expansion of the short-term GMMAs suggest that the secondary trend momentum is increasing. There is more "Buying or Selling" in the direction of the trend. See Figure 8.

Figure 8: Compression and Expansion of Short-term GMMAs

- ❏ Periods of compression of the long-term GMMAs (when the GMMAs narrow down) suggest that the momentum of the primary trend is fading. This means that the trend is weakening, and we should be prepared to tighten our stops.
- ❏ Periods of expansion of the long-term GMMAs suggest that the momentum of the primary trend momentum is increasing. There is more "Buying or Selling" in the direction of the trend. This is the sign of a strong trend. See Figure 9.

Figure 9: Compression and expansion of Long-term GMMAs

❏ The short-term GMMAs will fluctuate, but while the long-term GMMAs are in a steady band (i.e., with good separation) it suggests a steady trend with a low probability of collapse. Sustained activity of the short-term GMMAs above (or below) the long-term GMMAs confirms a strong trend. See figures 10 and 11.

Figure 10: Angle and separation and expansion of long-term GMMAs shows continued strength in trend

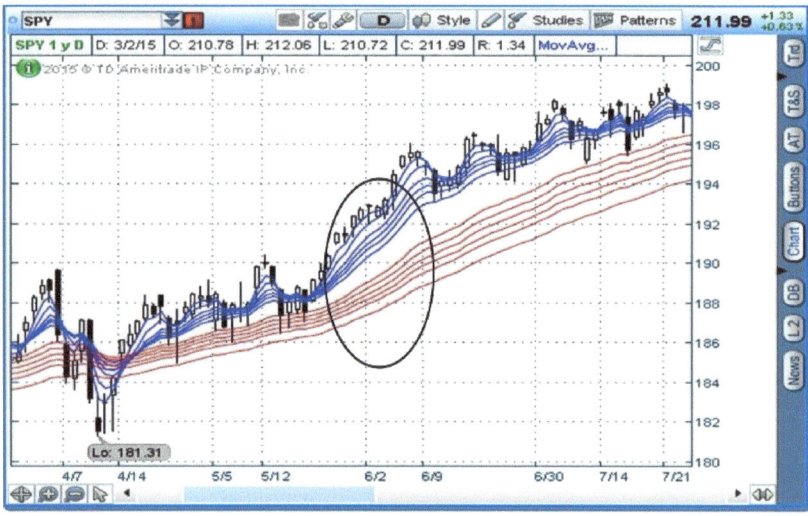

Figure 11: Angle and separation and expansion of long-term GMMAs shows continued strength in trend

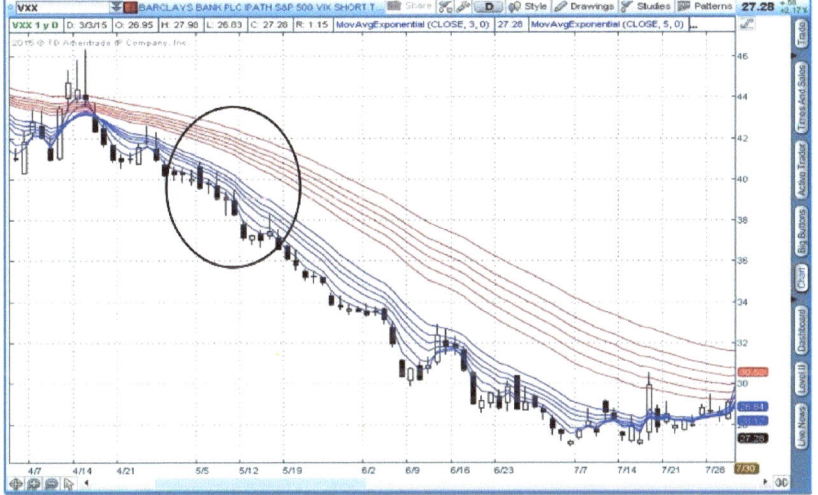

❑ When the two groups of moving averages narrow down (compression phase) and fluctuate more than is normal given their past recent activity, the trend is about to end. If the short-term GMMA penetrates the long-term GMMA, then a trend reversal is signaled. See Figure 12.

Figure 12: Penetration Phase

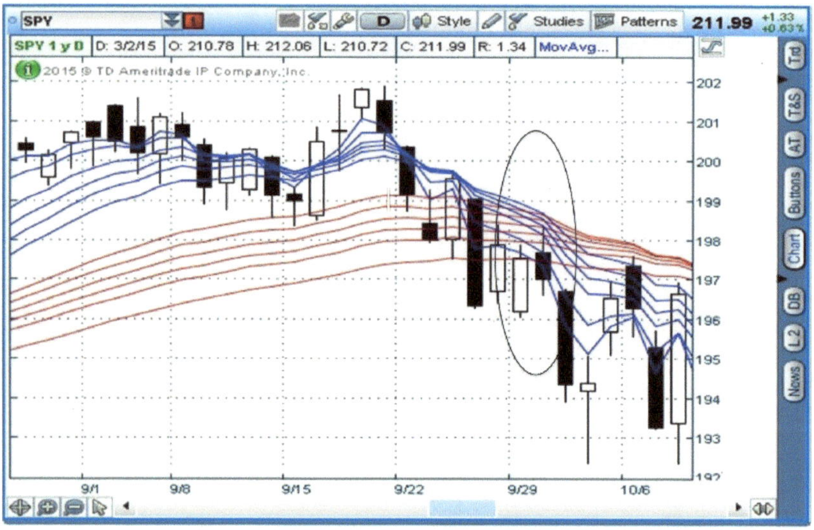

❏ The braiding/weaving pattern occurs when there is no angle and separation between the two groups of GMMAs. Do not trade during braiding/weaving. Wait for the opportunity to trade breakouts. See Figure 13.

Figure 13: Do NOT trade during Braiding/Weaving wait for breakouts

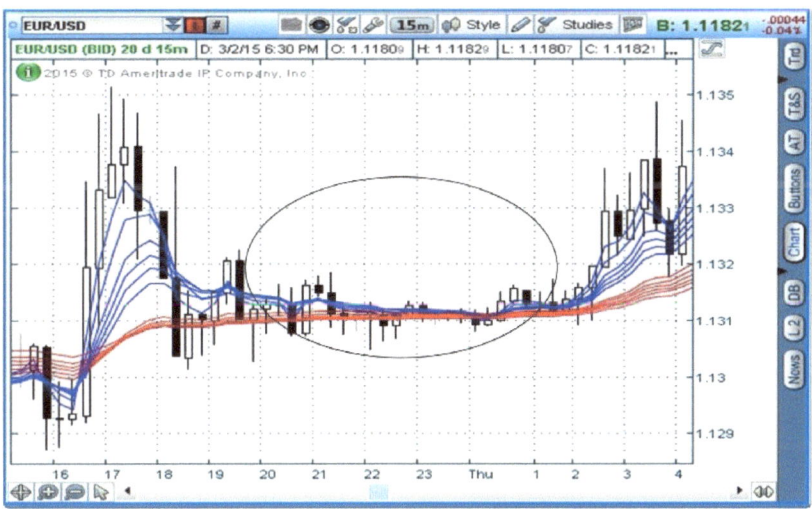

Full Stochastic Oscillator

As you may recall, the system uses two stochastic oscillators - long-term STO and short-term STO. I use the long-term STO as a cycle indicator to time the cycles on the primary trend and the short-term STO for the secondary trend. For each STO, I look at position and slope of the %D line to determine cycle stage for the respective trends:

- %D below 20 - cycle bottom
- %D above 20 below 80 and increasing - cycle up
- %D above 20 below 80 and decreasing - cycle down
- %D above 80 - cycle top

Relative Strength Index

I use this indicator as a confirming indicator for the strategy. This is my momentum filter.

200 Exponential Moving Average

I use this moving average to determine the dominant trend of the market. The dominant trend is up when this moving average is sloping upward, and down if it is sloping downward. I also use this moving average to tell me the potential support and resistance zones.

Chapter 5
The Strategy – Methodology

Here is the trading methodology, briefly.

- The trading time frame is based on daily charts.
- We use the 200-day exponential moving average as an indicator to define the dominant trend of the market. If the 200 EMA is sloping upward, the dominant trend is up. If it is sloping downward, the dominant trend is down. Otherwise, it is sideways.
- We use the GMMA indicators to analyze the primary and secondary trends of the market.
- We only trade in markets with strong primary trends aligned with their dominant trends.
- The primary trend is strong if there is a good angle and separation between the moving averages in the long-term GMMAs.
- The trend is to be confirmed by a good angle and separation between the short-term and long-term GMMAs.
- An entry signal is generated when the trend and cycle of the secondary trend align with that of the primary trend. An exit signal is generated when they are out of alignment. See Figure 14.
- A trailing stop is used to cut losses and protect profits against unanticipated reversals.

Figure 14: Alignment of Primary and Secondary Trends and Trend Cycles

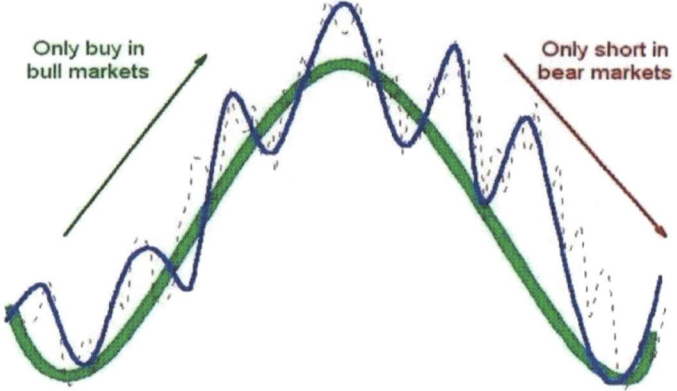

Chapter 6
The Strategy - Trading Rules

Entry Criteria

- The market must be in a strong primary trend—the moving averages within the long-term GMMAs must have a good angle and separation.
- There is a good angle and separation between the short-term and long-term GMMAs to confirm the overall trend.
- The primary trend must be aligned with the dominant trend as indicated by the slope of the 200-day exponential moving average.
- Price action must not be heading for the 200 EMA or long-term GMMAs.
- Only buy or sell with the trend. Buy dips in an uptrend and sell rallies on a downtrend.
- Buy or sell when both the short-term STO and long-term STO are pointing in the same direction of trade with the short-term GMMAs show a good angle and separation.
- Confirm with RSI—RSI must rise above 50 on a buy and decline below 50 on a sell.
- Use 60 EMA as a trailing stop.

Example 1 shows a buy entry active on 1/22/2015 for the currency pair AUD/USD. Let's review how each of the criteria applies:

- ❏ Long-term red GMMAs are showing good angles (down) and are separating, indicating that the primary trend is in a strong downtrend.
- ❏ There is a good angle and separation between the short-term and long-term GMMAs, with the short-term GMMA lying below the long-term GMMA, confirming the downtrend.
- ❏ The primary trend aligns with the dominant trend which is down.
- ❏ The direction of the trade is for the market to move away from the long-term GMMAs and the 200 EMA.
- ❏ We are selling rallies on a downtrend.
- ❏ The short-term STO and long-term STO are pointing in the same direction of the trade. The short-term GMMA is showing a good down angle and separating.
- ❏ This is confirmed by the RSI as it is passing below 50 from above.
- ❏ Set trailing stop at the 60 EMA level (0.8352).

Example 1: AUD/USD Sell Entry on 1/22/15

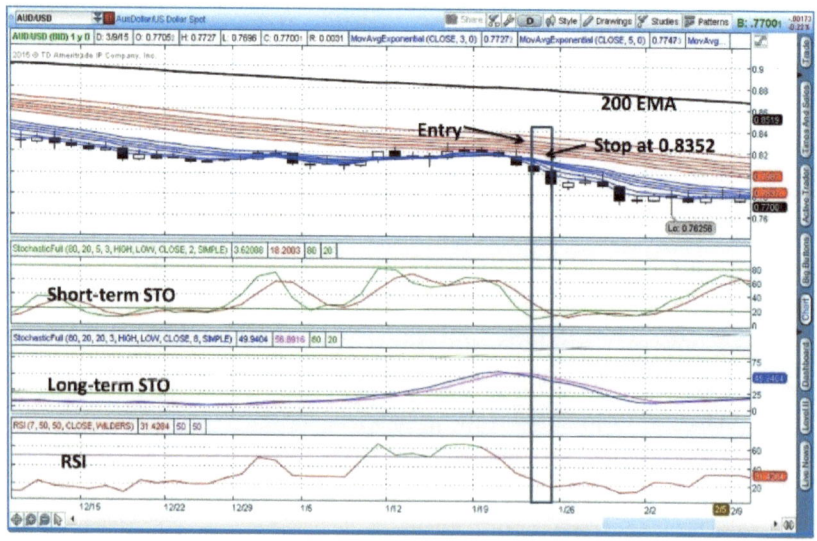

Exit Criteria

- Exit when both the short-term and long-term STOs are going in the opposite direction of trade
- Confirm with RSI moving in the opposite direction past the 50-level line
- When the above happens, get out on the next open or tighten your stop to let the market take you out

Example 2 shows an exit signal on 12/9/14 for the spy ETF. The trade was entered back in 10/21/14. Let's review how each of the criteria applies:

- Both the short-term STO and the long-term STO are moving in the opposite direction of trade
- This was confirmed by the RSI passing below 50 from above.
- We will exit at the open the following day.

Example 2: spy exit on 12/9/14

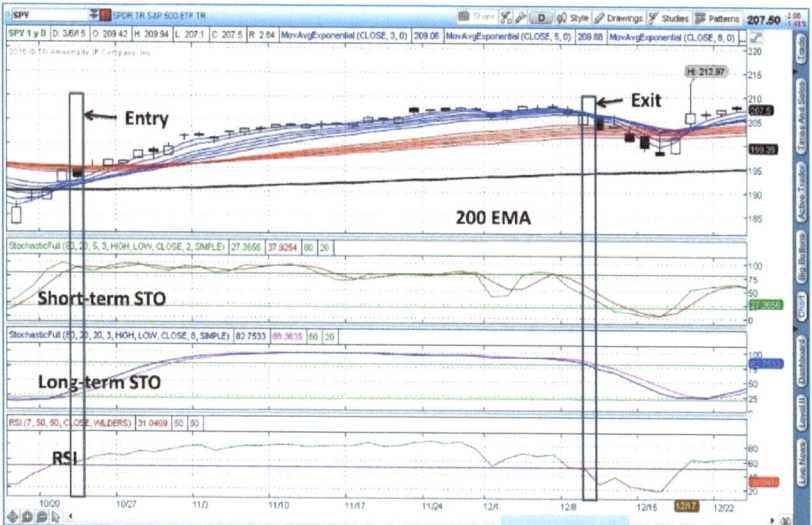

Example 2 also shows how the use of the RSI filter will prevent us from taking profits too soon. In this chart, we can see that both the short-term and long-term STOs are in the overbought zone for a while before the exit signal is generated. When both STOs are overbought, the market is in a stable and strong uptrend. Sometimes both STOs were pointing down prior to the exit signal, but the RSI remained bigger than 50 which prevented us from exiting the profitable trade too early. We only exit the trade when both the STOs are pointed down and confirmed by the RSI moving below 50 from above.

A Note About the Trailing Stop

We use the 60-day EMA to set our trailing stop to make sure that it is far away from the price action to prevent us from exiting too soon due to market shakeouts, but close enough in the sense that if the stock hits that level, the short-term GMMAs will cut into the long-term GMMAs, which is a warning signal for the market reversal. Under normal circumstances, if the trend is strong and stable, this is very unlikely to happen, and we will only need to follow the exit signal generated by the system.

Caution About Selling Short

If you are trading forex pairs or futures contracts, going short is as natural as going long. However, the same is not true for stocks and ETFs. Some stocks and ETFs are hard to borrow, making it almost impossible to sell short. More importantly, there are substantial margin requirements for selling short. In addition, you might lose more than the cash you received from selling short if you are wrong. Borrowed securities are subject to margin calls and recalls, forcing the short-seller to buy back the short, probably at the worst time. For these reasons, don't short stocks or ETFs. Instead, go long on inverse ETFs to gain market exposure to the downside. Inverse ETFs are available for most major market indices and a growing number of market sector funds. Another conservative way to get short exposures to securities is to use options, but that is out of the scope of this book.

Chapter 7
Diversification and Position Sizing

When you swing trade and keep positions overnight, I recommend you spread your money into multiple markets. Diversification is preferable to having "all your eggs in one basket." But we don't diversify just for diversification. We will only do this when we find valid setups. However, we're always looking for those valid setups. Therefore, I am always reviewing my watch list which is pre-designed with a wide variety of markets uncorrelated with each other.

So what type of markets are we watching that will help us diversify?

- Stock market sectors and industries
- Currencies
- Indexes of countries from around the world
- Bond ETFs
- Metals (gold, silver, etc.)
- Energy (oil, natural gas, gasoline, etc.)

Position Sizing

With diversification, naturally follows the question of position sizing. If I want to hold positions in multiple markets concurrently, how much should I invest in each one? There are many ways to position the size of your trades. I recommend that you limit 20% of your trading equity and risk only 3% of total equity in each trade.

Capital	= $100,000
Stock Price	= $50
Position Size	= $100,000 * 20% = $20,000 position / $50 price = 400 shares
Risk to Stop	= 3% * $100,000 = $3,000 / 400 = $7.50 stop, or $42.50 stop price

Chapter 8
Finding the Best Market to Trade

There are two ways to find the best markets to trade - (1) we scan for stocks that match our technical setups criteria, and (2) we create a watch list of major markets and measure their relative strength.

Scanning the Market for Setups

As Jim Cramer used to say, "*There is always a bull market somewhere.*" But how do you find it? Some brokerage platforms provide their customers with a facility to scan the market for setups. If your broker doesn't provide that facility, you can use an on-line scanning website such as **StockFetcher**. I recommend this website because:

- ❏ It's very inexpensive ($8.95/month).
- ❏ It doesn't matter what charting platform you use.
- ❏ It can scan daily and weekly charts simultaneously.
- ❏ It returns scan results blazingly fast.
- ❏ It comes with good charts.
- ❏ The "programming" language is very user-friendly and intuitive.

You can go to their website http://www.StockFetcher.com and test drive it. Below is an example of a scan so you can see how to write a scan.

GMAA Scan Code for a Long Setup in an Uptrend:

Show Stocks where EMA(15) is above EMA(30)
and EMA(30) is above EMA(60)
and EMA(200) is increasing
and the Stochastic %K(5,3,2) is increasing
and the Stochastic %K(20,3,8) is increasing
and the Average Volume(90) is above 100000
and close is between 10 and 100

IMPORTANT: The scans filter the universe of stocks down to a selected few meeting certain key elements we look for in our setups. Before taking any trade based on the scanned results, you must pull up a chart of the market and make sure it has a good setup.

Measuring Relative Strength

This is my favorite approach to finding the best markets to trade in and I'm constantly watching for this. When trading relative strength plays, I prefer to use forex pairs and Exchange Traded Funds (ETFs) rather than individual stocks. Stocks are subject to news, rumors and investor knee-jerk reactions that may not be sustainable or significant enough to trade.

There are several ways to find relative strength plays:

Stock Fetcher Formula:

Scan for ETF Relative Strength to S&P

show stocks where market is ETF
and the comparative relative strength(^SPX,90) is above 1.0
and compare with ^SPX
and the Average Volume(90) is above 200000
and close is between 5 and 100

Use a Relative Strength Scanner

There are several ETF Relative Strength scanner websites to do your RS Scan.

❏ **ETFTable** - This website uses two approaches to determine RS. One is on percentage performance and the other is based on EMA Crossover (% of fast over slow). Their beta version is free, and you can test drive it at http://www.etftable.com/.

❏ **ETFReplay Screener** - The ETFReplay screener is a statistical model that ranks ETFs according to the Relative Strength. The model has 3-factors: 2 timeframes for returns and 1 timeframe for volatility. You can register to be a free member that allows you to do RS Screening on the largest 100 ETFs. The subscription fee for full membership is $34.99 per month. You can test drive their screener at http://www.etfreplay.com/screener.aspx.

IMPORTANT: Before taking any trade based on relative strength, you must pull up a chart of the market and make sure it has a good setup by itself, not just in relation to another market.

Chapter 9
Putting It All Together

Emotion is your enemy in trading. You must use a methodical approach to trading to keep emotions on track. That's why we trade using the daily timeframe, so all trading decisions are made outside of market hours when the constant flow of changing price information has been temporarily turned off until the next session. Here is how I keep things simple and sweet.

Daily Routines

I will spend no more than thirty minutes on these daily routines. I will not go through these routines when the market is open. I will do it after the market closes.

- ❏ Review the order status of all trade orders set up with the broker for that day to see which ones are filled and which are not.
- ❏ Review the charts on markets I have positions on to see if there are exit signals and/or if I need to adjust or tighten the trailing stops. I will enter the required orders into the brokerage platform for execution the next trading day. For exits, I normally use market orders, so I can guarantee I can exit my position the next day.

- ❏ Review charts on my watch list to see if there are any new setups. If I have new setups, I will calculate how many shares to trade based on my position sizing criteria. Then I will enter the new orders into the system for execution the next trading day. For entries, I will use a limit order at a price close to the market. If it doesn't get filedl the next day, I will let the order expire. There may be better markets to trade with the next day.
- ❏ If I have more time that day, I may scan the market for trade setups. If there are suitable candidates, I may want to initiate a trade on that asset, or put it on my watch list for the future.

Weekly Routines

- ❏ Review the charts of all positions to ensure the trends are still running strong.
- ❏ Update the watch list to add markets with higher relative strength and delete markets that are not performing well.

TO SUCCEED AT trading, you must get in tune with the market rather than impose your own set of beliefs upon them. The longer-term outperformance of a trader comes from the preservation of capital during times of market uncertainty and then having that capital ready to deploy when the market presents conditions that favor your approach. If the market does not provide a clear direction, the correct interpretation should be to sit on the sidelines and preserve capital until the low-risk opportunities present themselves. You only need a handful of strategies to attain consistent trading profits. To have more only confused the issue.

I hope you enjoy reading this book and adopt the strategy for your own use. Plan your trade and trade your plan.

What Next?

I recommend you paper trade this strategy for a month before trading with your hard-earned money. To paper trade means to simulate buying and selling securities without using real money. It is a form of practice trading. You do all the trades following the rules of my strategy on paper. Do not use cash. It is a practice and it will help you feel confident when you make your first real trade. Do not fudge and front run the system. Pretend the family farm is on the line. Do several of these paper trades the first month, sit back, and watch what happens. If you can put yourself in a position where you feel like your family nest egg is on the line, you might find that the stress is not for you. If so, trend-trading is not for you.

While doing your practice trades on paper, remember these rules.

- Plan your trade and trade your plan.
- Trade only if the security is trending strongly and be on alert if the trend is fading.
- Do not trade a countertrend.
- Cut your losses short and let your winners run.
- Do not day trade on small timeframes.
- Diversify your portfolio using uncorrelated assets.
- If there is no trade setup, stay on the sideline and keep your powder dry so you can to be ready for the next trading opportunity.

I have repeated the rules to make sure you understand them. There is a fine line between winners and losers in the market. The trader on the opposite side of your trade is probably smarter than you are, has more software on his computer, and subscribes to ten "stock-tips." However, you have rules and guidelines that work. Follow them, and the odds are that you will succeed.

I wish you the best of luck and happy trading.

Lee Tang

About the Author

Lee Tang is a retired executive of a major global insurance company. Prior to his retirement, he has worked as an actuary, a risk officer and a chief financial officer for several major insurance organizations in the United States, Canada, and Taiwan.

Plea from the Author

Hey, Reader. So you got to the end of my book. I hope that means you enjoyed it. Whether or not you did, I would just like to thank you for giving me your valuable time to entertain you. I am blessed to have such a fulfilling job, but I have that job only because of people like you; people kind enough to give my books a chance and spend their hard-earned money buying them. For that, I am eternally grateful.

If you would like to discover more about my other books then please visit my website for full details. You can find it at https://lmtpress.wordpress.com.

Also feel free to contact me by email (leetang888@gmail.com), as I would love to hear from you.

If you enjoyed this book and would like to help, then you could think about leaving a review—even if it's only a line or two—on your favorite bookstore, Goodreads, or other sites; and talk about the book with your friends. The most important part of how well a book sells is how many positive reviews it has, so if you leave me one then you are directly helping me to continue this journey as a full-time writer. Thanks in advance to anyone who does. It means a lot.

Lee Tang

Also by Lee Tang

Standalones

Dual Momentum Trend Trading: *How to Avoid Costly Trading Mistakes and Make More Money in the Stock, ETF, Futures and Forex Markets with This Simple and Reliable Swing Trading Strategy.*

Canada's Public Pension System Made Simple: *The Secrets To Maximizing Your Retirement Income From Government Pensions*

Summary & Study Guide Series

1. **Summary & Study Guide - Brain Maker:** *The Power of Gut Microbes to Heal and Protect Your Brain-Including Diet Cheat Sheet*
2. **Summary & Study Guide - The Gene:** *An Intimate History*
3. **Summary & Study Guide - The Emperor of All Maladies:** *A Biography of Cancer*
4. **Summary & Study Guide - NeuroTribes:** *The Legacy of Autism*
5. **Summary & Study Guide - Brain Storms:** *The Race to Unlock the Secrets of Parkinson's Disease*
6. **Summary & Study Guide - The End of Diabetes:** *The Eat to Live Plan to Prevent and Reverse Diabetes-Including Diet Cheat Sheet*
7. **Summary & Study Guide - The End of Heart Disease:** *The Eat to Live Plan to Prevent and Reverse Heart Disease-Including Diet Cheat Sheet*
8. **Summary & Study Guide - ADHD Nation:** *Anatomy of An Epidemic - Attention-Deficit/Hyperactivity Disorder*
9. **Summary & Study Guide - The Obesity Code:** *Unlocking the Secrets of Weight Loss*

10. **Summary & Study Guide - How Not to Die:** *Discover the Foods Scientifically Proven to Prevent and Reverse Disease*
11. **Summary & Study Guide - Mind over Meds:** *Know When Drugs Are Necessary, When Alternatives Are Better - and When to Let Your Body Heal on Its Own*
12. **Summary & Study Guide - A Crack in Creation:** *Gene Editing and the Unthinkable Power to Control Evolution*
13. **Summary & Study Guide - The Gene Machine:** *How Genetic Technologies Are Changing the Way We Have Kids - and the Kids We Have*
14. **Summary & Study Guide - The Body Builders:** *Inside the Science of the Engineered Human*
15. **Summary & Study Guide - Into the Gary Zone:** *A Neuroscientist Explores the Border Between Life and Death*
16. **Summary & Study Guide - Fat for Fuel:** *A Revolutionary Diet to Combat Cancer, Boost Brain Power, and Increase Your Energy-Including Diet Cheat Sheet*
17. **Summary & Study Guide - The Alzheimer's Solution**: *A Breakthrough Program to Prevent and Reverse Cognitive Decline at Every Age*
18. **Summary & Study Guide - Healing Arthritis:** *Your 3-Step Guide to Conquering Arthritis Naturally*
19. **Summary & Study Guide - Rise of the Necrofauna:** *The Science, Ethics, and Risks of De-Extinction*
20. **Summary & Study Guide - We Are Our Brains:** *A Neurobiography of the Brain from the Womb to Alzheimer's*
21. **Summary & Study Guide - The Teenage Brain:** *A Neuroscientist's Survival Guide to Raising Adolescents and Young Adults*
22. **Summary & Study Guide - The Better Brain Solution:** *How to Reverse and Prevent Insulin Resistance of the Brain, Sharpen Cognitive Functions, and Avoid Memory Loss*

23. **Summary & Study Guide - The Plant Paradox:** *The Hidden Dangers in "Healthy" Foods That Cause Disease and Weight Gain*
24. **Summary & Study Guide - The Fountain:** *A Doctor's Prescription to Make 60 the New 30*
25. **Summary & Study Guide - Resurrection Science:** *Conservation, De-Extinction and the Precarious Future of Wild Things*
26. **Summary & Study Guide - Sapiens:** *A Brief History of Humankind*
27. **Summary & Study Guide - Homo Deus:** *A Brief History of Tomorrow*
28. **Summary & Study Guide - The Beautiful Cure:** *Harnessing Your Body's Natural Defences*
29. **Summary & Study Guide - The Diabetes Code:** *Prevent and Reverse Type 2 Diabetes Naturally*
30. **Summary & Study Guide - Brain Food:** *The Surprising Science of Eating for Cognitive Power*
31. **Summary & Study Guide - Anticancer Living:** *Transform Your Life and Health with the Mix of Six*
32. **Summary & Study Guide - The End of Epidemics:** *The Looming Threat to Humanity and How to Stop It*
33. **Summary & Study Guide - The Rise and Fall of the Dinosaurs:** *A New History of a Lost World*
34. **Summary & Study Guide - 10% Human:** *How Your Body's Microbes Hold the Key to Health and Happiness*
35. **Summary & Study Guide - The Mind-Gut Connection:** *How the Hidden Conversation Within Our Bodies Impacts Our Mood, Our Choices, and Our Overall Health*
36. **Summary & Study Guide - Civilization:** *The West and the Rest*
37. **Summary & Study Guide - Microbia:** *A Journey into the Unseen World Around You*
38. **Summary & Study Guide - An Elegant Defense:** *The Extraordinary New Science of the Immune System*

39. **Summary & Study Guide - Cancerland**: *A Medical Memoir on Cancer and Stem Cell Research*
40. **Summary & Study Guide - Empty Planet**: *The Shock of Global Population Decline*
41. **Summary & Study Guide - The Longevity Paradox**: *How to Die Young at a Ripe Old Age*
42. **Summary & Study Guide - Eat to Beat Disease**: *The New Science of How Your Body Can Heal Itself*
43. **Summary & Study Guide - The Tangled Tree:** *A Radical New History of Life*
44. **Summary & Study Guide – The Body:** *A guide for Occupants*
45. **Summary & Study Guide - The Spectrum of Hope:** *An Optimistic and New Approach to Alzheimer's Disease and Other Dementias*
46. **Summary & Study Guide - Memory Rescue:** *Supercharge Your Brain, Reverse Memory Loss, and Remember What Matters Most*
47. **Summary & Study Guide – The Longevity Code:** *Secrets to Living Well for Longer from the Front Lines of Science*
48. **Summary & Study Guide – Healing Anxiety and Depression**
49. **Summary & Study Guide - Healing ADD/ADHD:** *The Breakthrough Program that Allows You to See and Heal the 7 Types of ADD/ADHD*
50. **Summary & Study Guide - The Telomere Miracle:** *Scientific Secrets to Fight Disease, Feel Great, and Turn Back the Clock on Aging*
51. **Summary & Study Guide - The Finance Curse**: *How Global Finance Is Making Us All Poorer*

For a complete list of books by Lee Tang and information about the author, visit *https://lmtpress.wordpress.com*.

www.ingramcontent.com/pod-product-compliance
Lightning Source LLC
Chambersburg PA
CBHW041107180526
45172CB00001B/153